ESCOFFIER:
KING OF CHEFS

Owen S Rackleff

BROADWAY PLAY PUBLISHING INC
224 E 62nd St, NY, NY 10065
www.broadwayplaypub.com
info@broadwayplaypub.com

Cover art by Tom Van Herwarde

First edition: January 1983
This edition: May 2017
I S B N: 978-0-88145-000-2

Book design: Marie Donovan
Play text set in Baskerville by BakerSmith Type, N Y C
Printed and bound in the U S A

Owen S. Rackleff as Escoffier, at Hyde Park NY.

Escoffier: King of Chefs was first presented in The Theatre-at-St. Clement's, New York City, April, 1981 with the following cast:

Georges Auguste Escoffier . . . . .Owen S. Rackleff.

Directed by Laurence Carr
Scenery & Lighting by Peter Harrison
Costume by Linda Vigdor

Subsequent productions include: Hyde Park Festival Theatre, Hyde Park, N.Y.; The Cooper Union, New York City; the Chautauqua Amphitheatre, Chautauqua, N.Y.

Act One

The Setting: A pleasant airy room in the Villa Fernand, Monte Carlo; spring morning, 1922. A draped window in the rear; a desk with telephone and papers. Paintings are seen on the walls along with many photographs and awards. Downstage is an easy chair near a table, on which stand several framed photographs, a cup of tea, a bowl of fruit and some books and papers. Behind the chair is a covered oil portrait of a man (César Ritz)—unfinished—on an easel, with artist's supplies nearby.

GEORGES AUGUSTE ESCOFFIER, age 75, enters after a moment. He wears a silk dressing gown, cravat, black trousers and slippers. In his hand, he carries a few letters and telegrams. He glances at them, then, somewhat annoyed, turns to the audience:

ESCOFFIER

I am seventy-five years old; retired these past four years and they want me to go back to work. And I want to know if sixty years in and out of kitchens isn't enough! *(Looks at a letter in his hand.)*

"The King of chefs and the chef of kings", that's what they call me. I've already earned my reputation. Why put it in jeopardy now by trying to live up to it? *(Tosses the letter on his desk.)* Besides, I've this very pleasant villa here in Monte Carlo, where the weather's ideal. I can paint my little pictures, putter in the garden and hopefully complete that cookbook they've all been asking for.

(Picks up the letter, grudgingly.)

I can sleep; sleep late. Not be forced to get up before dawn and hurry to the markets. I can rest. *(Glancing at the photographs on his table, which include a large portrait of King Edward VII, in Coronation Robes, and others of Nellie Melba and Sarah Bernhardt.)*

After all those years with the likes of Melba, Bernhardt and Bertie—Bertie, our dear Edward VII, God rest him— after all that excitement, isn't it time, at last, for a little siesta?

Ah, no—but along come these letters and telegrams from Mme. Giroix, urging me, begging me, to go back to work. And who can blame her, poor lady? Newly widowed with a big hotel to run at the height of the season. And she probably figures how can I say "No" to the memory of her husband Jean Giroix. *(Reflectively)*

Jean had been my colleague, you know, from the time I first went to Paris, during the Franco–Prussian War, way back in 1870. That was the year of the awful Paris Siege. The damned Prussians were trying to starve us out, forcing a great many elegant restaurants to serve up animals auctioned at the local zoo! Even at the famous Café Voisin the menu boasted something called *Trompe Chasseur*, "Hunter's Trumpet", which was actually the trunk of an elephant—grilled! With mushrooms.

Jean and I knew a challenge when we saw it, even back in 1870. He learned to cook fifteen omelets from a single ostrich egg, while I had to disguise various cuts of kangaroo, also lately from the zoo, which, in the hands of a good sauce chef, should be no worse than any other game. But imagine: "Leg of Kangaroo"! I was terrified lest it start hopping away before I could braise it. My sauce, which had quite a little "kick" to it—if I must say so—did the trick. A perfect camouflage, especially with a sprinkling of truffles. As a result, *Ragout de Kangaroo* became the leading item on the menu for two whole days and I became second chief assistant to the associate chef!

Damn it all, if I didn't get a request for Kangaroo Stew ten years later when I was running my own little restaurant in Cannes! By then, Jean Giroix was here in Monte Carlo at the Grand Hotel cooking omelets—from the eggs of hens. When he decided to leave the Grand and needed a replacement, he very kindly recommended me to the general manager, a certain Swiss gentleman named César Ritz. Mme. Giroix was sure to remind me of that, clever lady.

(Reading from the letter): "Had it not been for Jean, you might

never have met César Ritz, God rest him—and that would have altered things a bit for you."

A bit! *(He tosses the letter on his table)* I was quite unprepared for any sort of change. Why should I have been? My own little restaurant in Cannes was flourishing—though I must confess I was not exactly a household name, despite *Ragout de Kangaroo.* Then, one day, into the foyer strolled César Ritz, impeccable as ever, demanding as ever, never content to relax or leave things as they were and promising great renown.

(He sits in the easy chair.)

My motto, I often told him: "Do it simply". His motto: "Do it with style". Putting on the Ritz, I think someone else called it. Would we ever be compatible?

Well, I must be a "pushover" for such things: style, renown, despite what I say. I moved to the Grand Hotel and before long was cooking up fancy egg dishes for none other than Queen Victoria, when she descended on the Riviera. The Grand became the *dernier cri* of Monte Carlo. And why? Well, Marie Louise, the wife of Ritz, once told me that he said it was all due to my cooking. In my opinion, it was his achievement. My friends, he took a crumbling old hotel and gave it elegance without ostentation and character without arrogance. Makes one long for the past to think of those warm and stylish surroundings; those sparkling tablecloths . . .

(Seems lost in memory, then begins to chuckle.)

Not like my old uncle's restaurant where I had my first job as a waiter. The tablecloths there were glorified floursacks. And the chef was a petty tyrant! I remember one day suggesting a simple decoration of sugared flowers for a fruit salad. I soon found myself looking for a new job.

(He reaches for his cup of tea and sips.)

I landed one at the Hotel Bellevue in Nice where lived this pale, sickly young lady unable to eat anything but cold breast of chicken. The problem: how to make it more appealing for her.

(Replaces the cup.)

Well, I remember, I was just an apprentice at the time, but I took it upon myself to experiment. Now, I've always loved pears. So I skinned one lightly, poached it a while in syrup, then let it cool. Cutting the pear into halves, I set a breast of cold chicken between the halves and garnished it with watercress. Then—to this day I do not know why—I dropped a little sugared violet in the center of it all and presented my creation on a crisp white linen napkin.

Hélène—for that was the invalid's name—responded joyfully. Ate it entirely, even wanted more. *Chicken Hélène,* I called it.

Turned out her father was a restaurateur in Paris. So to Paris I went, cooked my kangaroos, met Giroix and, yes, because of Giroix, met César.

César Ritz!

(He goes to the oil painting of Ritz and unveils it with pride.)

One day, at the Grand, he came to me: César—and announced that it was time for us to invent a few new dishes. *(in a Germanic accent:)* "The discovery of a new dish," he said, "does more for the happiness of mankind than the discovery of a star!" He was quoting that great old gourmand Brillat–Savarin. But of course I agreed. Always did, always will. And I must say I had been itching for years, since my *Chicken Hélène,* to develop something else of my own; something important that the world would notice. Because of César Ritz, I was soon to do just that and become a chef of fame. *(Catches sight of a photograph on the table.)*

Well—really it was Bertie's doing; the Prince of Wales, who insisted to his dying day that it was I who had caused the fashion for leaving the bottom button of the vest unfastened.

(Gruffly) "Can't button the damn thing anymore. And all your fault, Escoffier. All that delectable chicken pie. . ."

Old Bertie had a marvelous knack for causing things to happen indirectly. I suppose waiting all those years to become king gave him a sort of passive dynamism. Oh, but he could eat, no passivity there. Horse racing and food *and* the ladies were his true delights. But, above all food! So when he and his entourage—I think Lily Langtry was among them—descended on Monte Carlo to celebrate his winnings at the Derby, 1881, I created *Poularde Derby*, a famous dish which you may still find on a few good menus. And if not, you might like to try it at home. Although I warn you: my aim may be simplicity, but my recipes are fairly complex and you must never try shortcuts when it comes to stock. I don't care if it does mean boiling down three dozen chicken carcasses for 12 hours. Without a good stock—

(He breaks off, annoyed, and wearily walks back to his chair.)

Oh! but I'm not supposed to be thinking about cooking and menus and kitchens and stock! *(Sits wearily)* I'm not supposed to be thinking about anything actually, except rest and maybe poking at my pictures. Too much thinking and I'll be working for Mme. Giroix. Seventy–five years of age, gambling with my reputation.

(He sips some tea)

Ah, but that was a great recipe, my *Poularde Derby*. In the style of Carême, the master chef of Talleyrand; the true father of simplicity in cooking. "Every meat presented in its own natural juices. Every vegetable, just as God conceived it. . ."

I always take heart from what Alexandre Dumas wrote about Carême, always grow fiercely proud of my profession.

"Tell me, indeed," asked Dumas, "whether future generations will praise Napoleon more for Austerlitz or Carême for his invention of the Charlotte Russe?" *(Laughs)*

Mon Dieu, it's hard to be modest as a chef when you realize what joys, benefits, excitement you can bring to the world given half a chance. Delighting a little invalid or a paunchy prince. And delight him we did. Why, there was a tear in his eye, I swear, when he finished that *Poularde Derby*—the first serving. An actual tear!

(Rises suddenly and comes forward.)

Oh—get out your pencils! I'm too much a democrat to keep it only for His August Majesty. But don't tell Mme. Giroix that I'm spouting off recipes. She'll think I'm ready to surrender. Mustn't do that. César would laugh.

"Oh!" he'd say. "The old racehorse is growing tired of his pasture." *(Turns to the portrait, loudly)* No! I'm not. Not like César at least; always worrying, always. . .

(Studies the portrait a moment, then turns to the audience.)

But, I promised you *Poularde Derby.* Voila!

You stuff a small spring chicken with half—cooked rice, chopped truffles, foie gras and a dash of cream. Roast it slowly in butter, basting with a good white stock. Set the finished chicken on its dish and garnish with sautéed slices of foie gras on croutons crowned with whole black truffles, simmered in meat jelly, savored with champagne.

(He gently kisses his fingertips and crosses to his desk.)

Do you know, they tell me I have conceived nearly seven thousand recipes. Seven thousand! Many of them variations to be sure. Some of them as simple as *Oeufs Bernhardt,* for the "Divine Sarah": swiftly scrambled eggs prepared in a silver skillet. Some of them rather elaborate no doubt. My Grand Lobster Aspic in still considered *de rigueur* at state dinners in France, even by the Socialists. And while I'm on the subject: recipes and such, I must tell you about my delightful little "nymphs".

(Sits again, making sure no one is listening)

It was many years later in London, to which César had "abducted" me: the Savoy, that clever creation of Messrs. Gilbert and Sullivan. Well, not exactly *their* creation. "Their impresario, D'Oyly—Carte, decided to double his profits by building the Savoy Hotel nearby the theatre where Gilbert and Sullivan were packing them in.

Sated with *The Mikado* or *Pinafore,* the audiences were nonetheless starved for after—theatre meals. So, César took charge. The usual soft lighting in the dining room, the gleaming crystal, fresh flowers on the tables. But—a problem: refined ladies in those Victorian days in London never dined out. They barely allowed themselves to be seen at Gilbert and Sullivan. Clearly, César had to conceive a way of luring them to the new Savoy.

The Prince of Wales was enlisted—passively of course. *(In César's accent:)* "If Bertie will bring his ladies," César reasoned, "the others will follow. Especially if we create a brand–new dish, absolutely original, that will set them all agog."

"There is no absolutely original dish," I argued. "Even Ambrosia's been done."

"Oh, Auguste, mon petite maitr–rrr–e"—his Swiss accent intruding—"your mind is teeming with recipes. Come now. Something for the ladies. Just as the Prince would like it. We're counting on you. Musn't leave all the glory to Gilber–rrr–t and Sullivan!"

I suppose that pricked my artistic vanity, for I've always thought haute cuisine a definite art, the only indispensable one. An art certainly compared to: *(Singing)* "For I am called Little Buttercup, dear Little Buttercup. . ."* *(Shudders)*

Appeals to my pocket were useless. To my Art—Ah, well. Something for the ladies, eh? And who were they to be, these ladies? Well, Lily Langtry was definitely among them; Lady Randolph Churchill, the Countess de Frey—Bertie's usual "hunting party". What I created for them was *les cuisses de nymphes à l'aurore:* "The thighs of the nymphs at dawn." Nymph Thighs! Sounds delicious doesn't it? Exquisitely flavored titbits of meat in a pinkish–golden sauce, resting like chorus girls on a bed of tarragon.

"Excellent!" Bertie bellowed. "One might even say unique." *(Beckoning, softly)* "But what the devil is it anyway!"

César stood by, his eyes filled with anxiety. *(Muffled)* "What they don't know, won't harm them. . ."

Bertie continued: "The ladies are delighted. Your restaurant will be a haven for chattering females in no time. So—tell us the recipe, Escoffier. Modesty is ridiculous."

*From <u>H.M.S. Pinafore</u> by Gilbert and Sullivan.

Caution is not and I demurred. "Professional secret, Your Highness," I said, glancing at the unfastened button of his vest.

The next morning, however, came an urgent call from Marlborough House. The Prince demanded the nymph–thigh recipe—and demanded it now! Very well. I wrote it out.

(From a drawer—or shelf—in the table, he takes a toque, the traditional chef's hat, puts it on and closes the drawer.)

Always wear my toque when writing. *(Imitating writing, then miming the preparations:)* "Your Royal Highness: take two dozen frog's legs, poach in a court boullion until white. Prepare a seasoned cream and wine sauce with paprika, to resemble the color of dawn. Arrange the legs on a layer of champagne aspic to resemble the sea. Garnish with leaves of tarragon like seaweed and send to the table set on a block on ice."

(Rises explosively) "Frog's legs!!" The whole city of London practically trembled when the word got around. Many cockneys, who quite happily thrived on raw herring, gagged when told. Others, intrigued, flocked to the Savoy for a nibble. Before long every snob wanted his frog and I became famous as the man who taught England how to eat green amphibians. As a result, all Frenchmen were soon to be called "frogs"!

(Turns away indignantly.)

Well, what's in a name anyway. *Ragout de Kangaroo* comes immediately to mind. Properly cooked, anything may be palatable. César insisted horsemeat could be delicious, if properly prepared and I tend to agree, although it's oily. But he never said that *Ragout of Rat* was passable, even during the Siege of Paris!

(Laughs out loud, but then thinks better of what he's said.)

Now, lest some of *you* may be gagging, I hasten to redeem myself and César Ritz by describing a menu we presented in 1906 for the ten richest men in Paris, as a sort of culinary revenge for the indignities of *Trompe Chasseur*. The meal began at 8:30, at the Paris Ritz, ended at 11; average cost per person: four thousand francs. And yet it was fairly simple, simply served, no fanfares, and intended to please not to punish. I am happy to report that each of the guests slept like a top upon returning home and felt not the least indisposed upon arising. What more could I, or any chef, ask?

(Having sat, he begins in dreamy tones:)

We began with an amber consommé of pheasant, served in a silver cup—César loved silver. This, followed by a chiffon of Dover Sole topped with delicate herbs and artichokes. Sherry was served with the soup, Meursault with the sole. A fragrant stew of shelled crayfish tails was succeeded by creamy scallops of goose livers in nut–flavored sauce. To drink: Chateau Lafitte, 1870.

(Growing excited) The main course followed: breast of veal braised in cognac and cream, accompanied by a velvety purée of petit pois and sage–stuffed zucchini, with small roasted potatoes and crisp asparagus tips in golden butter. A sherbet refreshed the palate, along with Pommery and Grand Chambertin, 1900. Then—tender smoked woodcock, stuffed with its own liver. Ah, how Brillat–Savarin loved woodcock. Carried them around, freshly killed in his pockets until they reeked! Ours were garnished with tarragon and truffles cooked in paper envelopes. Frosted Mandarin oranges, rolled in shaved coconut and other delightful friands ended the meal, with fresh fruit, French cheese, a Chateau d'Yquem, 1869 and coffee—black as night, strong as death and hot as Love! *(Sighs wistfully.)*

Truly, as I often told César: "Beasts feed, man eats, but only the individual of intelligence and true perception really dines." On what did César dine that night? I think a cold chicken sandwich and a glass of Brioschi for his chronic indigestion. I retired to my room, had some consommé with rice, a pear and a toothpick flavored with peppermint.

(He removes his toque and places it on the table near Mme. Giroix's letter. He picks up the letter.)

Ah, but I'm rambling on about recipes and feasts and all

the rest like a man about to find himself back in harness, amid
the smoke and sputtering fat of some overblown hotel kitchen,
where appetite may be destroyed with a glance. No! *(Tosses
the letter on the table.)* Sorry Mme. Giroix. Much as you and the
ghost of old César would love to see me in uniform with skillet
and spoon, shouting orders, concocting variations of a variation and probably making a fool of myself, *I* prefer my quiet
villa, my good wife's cooking—which I still say is superior to
my own—my paintings and, damn them all, the memories.

(He looks at the many photos and citations on the walls.)

You can't escape the memories, can you? And I've usually
found that the most vivid memories of one's life are all woven
together somehow with—food.

That writer, Marcel Proust, who just died, poor fellow. He
took one bite of a Petite Madeleine biscuit dipped in lime–flavored tea and created six or seven *volumes* worth of
memories—from that one bite. Uncanny. But I think he was
right. Taste is a powerful force and memory a door that once
opened leads where?

(He picks up a book on the table.)

I was looking at my copy of Proust this week, hearing he
had died. We knew him. Strange, gaunt looking creature, the
color of wax. And no wonder. He used to hole himself up in
a sealed cork–lined room all day and only venture out at night,
most often to the Paris Ritz, where he'd sit reclusively in a
corner eating ices.

Here's what Proust wrote in his first book of memories:

(He finds the appropriate page in the book and reads:)

"When, from a long distant past, nothing subsists. After the
people are dead. After the things are broken and shattered.
Still alone, more fragmented, but with more vitality; more
un-substantial, more persistent, more faithful: the *smell and
taste* of things remain poised a long time like souls ready to
remind us, waiting and hoping for their moment, amid the
ruins of all the rest. . . "

(He closes the book reflectively.)

Hmm, after the people are dead. So many are gone now. I suppose only memory hangs around like a dinner guest never sated. And this fellow Proust is right. Too much memory and what happens? You find yourself where you don't want to be, where you've been already, been through it. Why, if I wanted to set down all the little things I could remember just by biting into a—a pear, I'd make *Proust* look "unsubstantial". *(He picks up a pear from the fruit bowl.)* And all about food and cooking and the people I've fed. It's people after all that give it life. I mean, what's a *Poularde Derby* left uneaten, causing no royal tear to be shed?

(Seems breathless and exhausted.)

But, I *must* rest. Time for siesta not recollection.
There are, now that I think of it, certain dangers in being a chef, getting too attached, too compulsive. Even a hotel manager. Could be fatal. Truly!

Take the case of Apicius, the master chef of ancient Rome, who took poison when he realized that he no longer had adequate funds to run his glorious kitchen.

Or, Vatel, poor Vatel, the chef of the Prince Condé in the time of Louis XIV. *(Rises and comes forward.)* When he learned that there was an insufficient amount of fish for the king's banquet, he put his sword in the door jamb of his room and after two ineffective attempts finally succeeded in the third in forcing the sword through his heart! *(Pause)*

I would have substituted white chicken meat for the missing fish. But—even so, I can understand Vatel's reaction.

(He bites into the pear, then stops short. Seeing the Giroix letters again, on the table, he emphatically tosses them into a wastepaper basket near his desk.)

Mind you, chefs these were. Not temperamental kings or opera stars. *(Lightening his mood)* Like—Mme. Nellie Melba.

(He picks up Melba's photograph from the table)

Alas, we are destined to go down in history as a team, I fear. Helen Mitchell of Melbourne, Australia—for Helen Mitchell was her original name—and Georges Auguste Escoffier of the Maritime Alpes. Why? Were we lovers? God forbid! I was far too fond of her for that. Enemies? Never. Not even when she accused me of seducing her appetite. No—we are bound together in the pages of a cookbook like—like bacon and eggs!

It was back in the days of the London Savoy and she was reigning queen of opera, singing everything from Marguerite in *Faust* to Elsa in Wagner's *Lohengrin*. I was in the audience at Covent Garden the night when she first tackled Wagner. Oh, she had wonderful moments to be sure. If only we could have done something about the *hours*. The real show followed at the Savoy where Nellie threw a fabulous bash, which I agreed to cater. Although, in typical prima donna fashion, it was *she* who tried to concoct the dessert.

(In a female voice:) "I want great masses of vanilla ice–cream shaped like the swan of *Lohengrin*," she ordered, "and at the last minute, flaming peaches are to be plunked around the base."

Well, I never like to plunk peaches or anything else, especially flaming, over an ice–cream swan, so I advised her quite soberly that hot peaches coming after a meal of Chateaubriand might be a bit offensive to the palates and tummies of those assembled, including several music critics. Poor Nellie had already offended those gentlemen quite enough with her Wagner, so she surrendered and with all the creativity I could muster, I did the following:

(Miming the following at his desk:) The peaches were poached in vanilla syrup, cooled, then nested on mounds of vanilla ice–cream. The whole was then glazed with strawberry jam—raspberry purée, which I prefer, came later. Each such ensemble was then "plunked", *set* , between the wings of a great ice–sculptured swan, which in turn sat upon a nest of spun sugar. *Swan Peaches*, I called it. Nellie added "Melba"; *Peach Melba!*

She also added quite a few pounds. You see, all that vanilla ice–cream and peaches hadn't helped the lady retain her so–called "out–back" figure. In fact, it was becoming decidedly more "out front" every day. As a result, we introduced her to one of César's creations. Actually, Mme. Ritz had required it for dieting: toast sliced in half. *(Nods)* Melba Toast, so called, which Nellie sampled maybe once or twice before returning to her beloved butter–drenched croissants—not to mention the plover's eggs *en croute* stuffed with caviar.

She was last in touch with me only a few years back, *Dame* Nellie, when I was also "knighted", made a Chevalier of the Legion of Honor in France. She sent a laudatory telegram simply signed "Peach Melba".

(He warmly kisses the photograph, and replaces it on the table.)

César, I fear, was always a little bit jealous of my relation-ships—culinary relationships—with these grand ladies of the stage, especially our dear Sarah Bernhardt. You see, cooking for people, giving them their little treats, is sort of like caress-ing them, or making love.

Sarah Bernhardt agreed: *(In a flowery voice:)* "Oh my dear Auguste, I am bored and I am unhappy and I am cross and I need either a new man, a new role, a new hat—or something from you."

"Well, what *about* a new hat," I'd say teasingly.

"No, cherie, no. One can only wear a hat, or a role, *or* a man. But a dish by Escoffier becomes a part of the soul".

Well, with such praise in my head I hardly knew what to do. César suggested boiling a ham. He could be nasty! *I* stuffed a chicken with rice in white sauce, poached it in cream, set it on a bed of toast and braised fennel, called it *Poularde La Tosca,* in honor of Sarah's most famous role—and crowned it with a crystallized violet just as I had done so long ago for that little invalid at the Hotel Bellevue *(Wistfully),* the one who thrived on my cold breast of chicken. It's my real trademark, I think: violets. Much more artistic than Melba Toast and far prettier.

César was also fond of floral touches. Witness his crisp white carnation changed every three hours. Witness the Ritz tables set with fresh flowers, an innovation at the time. And another: music for dancing conducted by Johann Strauss.

César also had a passion for the proper lighting effects. Mme. Ritz would pose for hours at the Savoy, later at the Carlton, under the lamps and chandeliers so that the correct light readings could be established. Bright enough by which to dine, without going blind. Dim enough to flatter the matron ladies.

In a word "Perfection", that was César's goal. *(He approaches the portrait.)* Time, order, these were his gods. Above all work! I was certainly devoted to my work, putting in twelve to fifteen hours a day when necessary. But César was a slave to his labors, often sleeping only three or four hours a night on his office couch. *(Growing upset)* Above all, he could not separate himself temperamentally from his task. Every bother became almost insurmountable for him. Why, he could become morose, personally wounded even by a housemaid's rudeness!

(At the desk.)

Often I tried to shake him from this compulsiveness, warning him it could result in nervous collapse. He scoffed at what he called my detachment. "It's got to hurt; it's got to hurt", he mumbled once when we were sweating out some ten–course banquet for 200 guests.

(Growing very angry)

"No!! It may be difficult, but it should always be fun". The kind of fun children have building sandcastles at the seashore. Anyway, as I've often said: Good cooking is the foundation of true happiness—so why not have some fun with it! *(Recovering)*.

That statement, by the way, is one of my better known quotes. Not that I consider myself such a wit. Although, there was that little exchange—made all the papers—with Wilhelm, better known as Kaiser Bill.

(Takes a sip of tea.)

It was aboard the SS Imperator, one of the great German

liners of its day where I'd been asked to supervise a banquet
for His August German Majesty. Remembering, of course,
that Wilhelm was Bertie's nephew and no doubt had similar
tastes and appetites, I offered as the main entrée a giant boned
salmon steamed in champagne.

"Excellent! Delicious!" The Kaiser bellowed after devouring
the fish. "You must come at *vonce*, Escoffier, and *verk* for
me in Berlin. I give you anything you desire!"

Horrified by the prospects of such an offer, I waited a
moment, smiled and replied: "Would Your Majesty consider
returning Alsace–Lorraine to France?" *(Laughs)*

Needless to say, I never went to Berlin.

César laughed hearing that little exchange. It was natural
a man of such taste and charm would also have a sense of
humor. *(He turns and studies the portrait.)* What was it then that
darkened him so, made him such a worry wart? He'd say: "I
know what my guests want *today*. But what will they want
tomorrow?"

I applied myself to the crises at hand. Today was enough
of a challenge. Getting to the markets early enough, for
instance, to make sure we got the best of the pick. That was
my passion. *(Sits)*

Otherwise, I tried to equate my temperament with the flavor
of a fine meal. Enough spice, enough sugar. Plenty of sub-
stance. All evenly and deliciously cooked and pleasantly
served, leaving only the most delightful aftertaste.

Of course, we both had our needs and our fantasies, César
and I. He could envision The Vatican converted into a ban-
queting hall. I, to this day, am still concocting recipes, especially variations on the simple things. Plotting a new assult on
the egg. An omelet worthy of a prince. *(Sighs sadly.)*

Ah, but they're all gone, the princes I knew. No need to
start all that up again. Leave it to the new breed. Let *them* be
blamed for ruining the stomachs and figures of their clientele,
though Lord knows I tried to spare mine. Especially King
Edward. Why, he could easily manage two dozen oysters at
eleven *AM* to "stave off" hunger between a breakfast of bacon,
kidneys, kippers and salad, and a lunch of quail, trout, cold

pigeon pies and deep bowls of sherbet with Angel Food cakes.

No wonder the poor man grew like a hippopotamus. Morning, noon, night and the times between would find him nibbling cheese or paté, gulping down oysters and clams, stuffing his cheeks with tarts and jellies and sending it all afloat with gallons of assorted beverages from Ginger beer to Dom Perignon!

Everyone thought it so amusing. How they loved their overgrown Teddy. "Tum–Tum", he was affectionately called. Very amusing, except to those who really loved him and cared for his health. Oh, Alexandra, his wife, thought it best to humor his appetites—all of them. His mother simply ignored him. César and I tried to offer some control. We cut down the fourteen–course dinners at the Carlton and stayed with seven in hopes our friend would benefit. Well—he ate our seven then trotted off to Rules or the Café Royale and put away another seven of theirs.

Little did we realize what all this would lead to; what a strange effect the royal appetite would have on our lives. Especially César's. It makes me feel odd all over even talking about it. Gives me pangs of guilt. Makes me question the virtues of my calling. Are we as chefs truly the "preservers of mankind", as we'd like to believe? Or do we harm as much as we benefit? *(Troubled)*

It's inevitable I suppose. A chef measures his success, his triumph, the way any other artist does. By acceptance. We are pained to think of people deprived of good food, well prepared—even if they do start to show signs of obesity. We weep for prince and pauper alike. *I* weep for everyone without taste or relish in his eating.

But I also weep for César and Bertie and—and even for myself. I am an old man, retired, in need of his rest and not of further recipes . . .

(Door chimes from the hall interrupt him)

What's that? *(He rises and tiptoes toward the window.)*
A visitor?

(He looks out of the window.)

Oh, no! Another telegram. Mme Giroix, I'll wager. Oh, that dear persistent lady.

(Ominously) And what a time to intrude. Just as I was talking about Bertie, the Carlton, César and the awful blow that fell upon us all. And what a blow . . .

(Door chimes again. He signals the audience to stay put, then turns to the door.)

Coming! Coming! . . .

(He starts off as the lights rapidly fade and the chimes ring once more, insistently.)

[END OF ACT ONE]

Act Two

Same setting, a few minutes after the end of Act One. Escoffier returns holding an unopened telegram.

ESCOFFIER *(Showing the telegram)*

Mme. Giroix, as I predicted. No need even to open it. How can I think of going back to work in the face of what happened. That awful blow which fell upon us all. *(Comes forward.)*

The old queen, you see, had breathed her last at Windsor in January, 1901. Albert Edward, after waiting nearly sixty years, was at last King of England. Our friend and patron. "Tum-Tum", who we had pampered and fed and fattened in spite of ourselves.

Of course, the new king was very fond of César Ritz, of the Carlton Hotel and, he told me often, of me and my cuisine, though I hardly think the two can be separated. It was, therefore, no surprise to anyone when the Palace announced that Edward's coronation feast, in June 1902, would take place at the Carlton as a sort of grand farewell to Bertie and a welcome to the Edwardian Age. César for once was overjoyed and full of plans

(Eagerly) I was not without my own plans and responsibilities, including a royal menu to create with items like lamb for Edward VII, chicken for Edward VII, quail and ham for Edward VII; salmon for Queen Alexandra and coupe after coupe after delicious coupe. Every detail was discussed in conferences at the palace. Ritz, Escoffier and Albert Edward himself busying each other with an agenda of "floral arrangements and wine lists." César was beside himself with anticipation.

Then the rumors began. The king wasn't eating, so his chef reported to the chef at the French Embassy who had reported the same to me. His Majesty had even cancelled a state banquet!

I was naturally surprised and perplexed. But, as was my habit, dismissed the gossip.

"It's just nerves and fatigue," I said as César paced his office. "You musn't get all knotted up."

(In César's voice:) "Oh, musn't I? Well suppose, just suppose . . ." He couldn't bring himself to say it.

"Suppose nothing! You're a perpetual worry wart, dear César. Enjoy your fame; enjoy the moment."

Well—*(He tosses the latest telegram on the table.)* What can I say? This time César was right. Two days before the Coronation I was summoned to his office at lunchtime—at *lunchtime* mind you. What could be wrong?

(Alternating César's voice and his own:)

"A bomb has fallen, Auguste!" He was very pale and shaken.

"A bomb! An actual bomb?"

"Worse than actual! There will be no Coronation. His Majesty is ill. Going into surgery . . ." Then he sank down in his chair and—sobbed.

I was frankly dismayed as a mountain of uneaten food suddenly loomed up in my imagination. But it was César not the food that mattered now.

(Gently, as though speaking to César).

"It will only be temporary. He'll recover. He's as strong as an ox, we've seen to that. A month, maybe two, it will all be as we planned."

(Shakes his head) No! César seemed to sense the worst.

"Things must happen, Auguste, when they're supposed to happen." He could never stand disorder or a change of plans.

(Walks toward the easel.)

Yet, in seeming control of himself, he placed a fresh carnation in his lapel, called together the staff, made the dire announcement—quietly, no outward emotion—then proceeded to the dining room to inform the luncheon crowd, which he did softly, darkly, amid deathly silence.

(Removing the painting from the easel, he gazes at it sorrowfully.)

For the next three hours César Ritz was nowhere to be found. Finally, at four PM, his carriage arrrived at his home, the driver trembling. M. César was slumped in the rear, unconscious, in a state of total collapse.

(He lays the portrait aside, face to the wall.)

The doctors called it a nervous breakdown. You might call it a broken heart. They ordered a long rest cure for him. No work, no worry for several months at least.

I went to my kitchens, had all the food packed and labeled and shipped off to a dozen hospitals. Even the lavish cakes, decorated in icing and wax flowers, went to the nuns and their orphanages.

At Buckingham Palace, meanwhile, the king was handling the crisis in his own way: fighting it tooth and nail. *But* an infected appendix complicated by obesity is a formidable foe and in the end he surrendered, had the operation and recovered to be crowned two months later.

(Points to the portrait.)

But César could not recover. The compulsion to work, the worries, the million concerns had taken their toll and fairly crippled him.

(Sits) Yet, to his amazement, the world went on. Even his *own* dominion. To me he entrusted completion of the new hotel near Green Park, the one that was to bear his name in London.

(Weakly, in César's voice:)

"You, Auguste, know what I expect," he told me from his bed. And as best I could, lacking his tyrannical flair, I saw to it that the new Ritz would indeed be worthy of the name.

And it was! It was a work of art, like its Paris counterpart. And the kitchen, so they said, was equally successful. By 1905, when the London Ritz opened, I had trained over two hundred master chefs, who went on to fill the great kitchens of the world, whether in private homes, grand hotels or on luxury liners. A one–man university, they called me. I who had never gone to school, except to art school as a boy. Escoffier's heritage in the persons of all those cooks. And the best were sent to the new Ritz kitchen.

Oh, we celebrated in style that day when the new hotel first opened its doors, not just for the enterprise, but for César, who had come from Switzerland to officiate. There he was, pale, shaking ever so slightly, the carnation in place, his eyes searching out the little imperfections: *(Slowly, weirdly in César's voice:)* "That chair clashes with that door. That vase in going to crack! . . ."

(Lost in sad contemplation.)

Within two months, he was bedridden once more. This time ordered not even to think. He hardly could. Thoughts and images blurred like fog in his mind. I could not bear what had happened to him, can hardly think of it now without the most awful mixture of sorrow and anger. Anger, yes! That he could not control those compulsive demons in him.

(Snatches up the telegram.)

That's why I get so angry at myself when I look at these endless telegrams and feel the same sort of compulsion starting up in me. The blow, or "bomb", which fell in 1902 and shattered poor César, left quite a few scars on me as well. Oh, the wasted food and the disappointments were incidental. What it had done to my partner and friend—*(Breaks off)*

But of course, we had to carry on. When the actual Coronation did take place, in *August* 1902, the Carlton played its part admirably. Not as lavishly, to be sure, as originally planned. But we managed, thanks especially to Mme. Ritz, God bless her. She had all of her husband's charm and taste, with none of his neuroses.

Of course, being without César did mean extra hours for me. It meant fewer visits to France. *(Takes up his tea cup.)* In fact, it meant that London, cold gray London, had at long last—and most unwillingly from my part—became home. For a dozen years I lived at the Carlton, then at the Ritz, like any Lord. And I daresay I took on English habits as well. *(Indicates the cup.)* After all, I was always in the company of Englishmen. Counted many among my closest friends.

Lord Chalfont best among them—and the most British of them all. Knew everyone, went everywhere. Full of good humor and stories, but, oh so sadly lacking in a taste for haute cuisine. Typical Englishman.

(Sips tea, chuckling, then sets the cup aside.)

One day, as he entered the dining room, Chalfont, looking for all the world like a well–dressed walrus, he called me to his side and said:

"If you want to make me 'appy, fix me up some "Star–Gazy Pie!"

"Star–Gazy Pie? Never heard of it," I confessed.

He smiled wickedly, happy I suppose to see me stumped and went on to describe a ghastly concoction from Cornwall, *(miming the words)* in which large herrings, raw, are piled up in a pie crust with all their heads joined in the center of the pile so that the topping can be laid around them revealing only their dull, dead eyes "gazing" through a hole in the center. Star gazing, you see. Stomach turning is more like it.

(Turns his eyes to King Edward's photograph on table.)

It was Chalfont who first brought me news that the king was dying, in May 1910. A month or so before I had supervised a royal picnic, like the old days. Bertie gorging himself then nodding off. The pretty ladies lowering their voices so that he could sleep.

When his doctors ordered him to bed, he complained: "I must go on working." Like César, I fear, our king was painfully compulsive. He was working on his engagement book, in fact, when he fell to the floor. Two days later, the Edwardian Age came to an end.

I called César in Lucerne. But he was unable to comprehend. My two dear friends: the king, age 69; César in his 50s. Burnt out, worked out—who can say what. *(Quiet pause.)*

But—it was time to think of other things. A new king's coronation and the Carlton all ablaze for the big festivities.

(Rises) Ablaze is the word! Not long after King George was crowned, the whole Carlton kitchen went up in fire, started in a rotisserie where a chicken had been left unattended. What an event! We all clambored to the hotel roof for safety while below the press shouted questions:

(In a loud voice:) "How do you explain the disaster, M. Escoffier?"

(Looking downward) "Disaster?" I asked. "Is everything in England a disaster?" Not as I saw it. *(Addressing the "press")* "For years we've been roasting chickens. It's about time one of them took revenge!" *(Laughs heartily.)*

That pompous Wilhelm, the Kaiser—who had so enjoyed my boned salmon—also saw fit to take revenge. For Lord knows what. Maybe for his shriveled arm, which he always blamed on "Mein English bluud". In any event, for four long years the Great War raged. In the kitchen the overly lavish feast and frill seemed somehow out of place. Happily, we never had to resort to *Ragout de Kangaroo* from the local zoo.

(Going to his desk.)

Just before the Armistice, when all of England and France felt hope and joy, the news came that César—so long in darkness—had finally passed over to what I pray is an eternity of peace and light. I remember Marie Louise's letter to me at the time. "He taught the world a new way of living," she said. "A better one than it had ever known."

I had, of course, seen César on and off during all those years of his infirmity, since that "bomb" of 1902. I had seen him fading as a man. But, I had also only to look around me at the Carlton, at the Ritz, at a dozen places where his influence had taken hold, to know that this nervous little man had achieved an immortality unique in his time.

(Energetically) Why, do you know, his *name* appears in the dictionary as a word: "ritzy", which according to those silly people means: "snobby, ostentatious, putting on a show!" Well, if that isn't far off the mark concerning César, what is?

I suppose it's like what's happened to Christmas. Ostentation was the very last thing César desired or allowed. Why, in Paris, at the Place Vendôme, the Ritz Hotel stands in magnificent—simplicity. The only elaboration can be found in the flowers; nature's own "ostentation."

How can it be that his name has been so bastardized? Like mine, I suppose, with a bottled concoction called "Sauce Escoffier." But at least that pays me a royalty.

What's in a name, after all? Peach Melba, Melba Toast—is that how Nellie is to be remembered? Ironic! Peach Melba goes on every day fattening and delighting people who never heard a note of opera in their lives. And in the same way, Marie Louise once wrote me that she overheard some tourist—American, I think—in the lobby of the Paris Ritz astonished to find a portrait there of César. "You mean there really was a man named Ritz? I thought it was only a cracker!" *(Amused)*

In that same letter Marie Louise also suggested that it was time I returned home, to Paris at least. France had decorated me, honored me, put me up there with the famous writers and diplomats.

(Reading from a framed citation on the wall:)

"Our finest ambassador of taste and tradition." So said the President of the Republic about me—me, an "ambassador"!

Well, as Dumas said: Cooking for politicians in whose hands the fate of nations is committed is a solemn *and* diplomatic duty.

Remember, I almost caused an incident with the Kaiser, about Alsace–Lorraine. Which in fact we did get back, didn't we? *(Winks)*

I personally do not have a political temperament and look upon history as a background for good dining—or poor dining, depending on one's luck. *(At his desk)* Even so, the World War meant tragedy for me, as for so many others. A son killed at the Marne . . .

(He takes up a framed photo of a young soldier and studies it quietly.)

César's death, my son's, the whole change that came over

the world, unnerved me, made me cranky. I began to resent
the London fog and grayness. Even old friends like Chalfont
and Melba and my colleagues in the kitchen could not appease
me. Clearly, it was time to go home. *(Replaces the soldier photo
on the desk.)* Marie Louise urged me to stay at the Paris Ritz
to help her son, Charles. But I kept remembering the warm
light and tranquility of the Riviera. I had my roots here, my
little villa and, above all, Delphine. Oh yes—Mme. Escoffier!

(To "someone" in the audience.)

   No, I was not married to my stove or my stockpot—or my
recipes. For nearly forty years, Delphine has been my help
and support, though often at long distance. She has wisely
preferred this climate to the drizzles of London and Paris.
Has lived here at the Villa Fernand, quietly, patiently, some-
times feeling abandoned no doubt. Little did she realize, way
back in 1884, when we married, that a restaurateur and chef
could have so hectic a life as I've had. She scolded me once:
   (In a brittle voice:) "You are not Caruso or Charlie Chaplin.
Why must you always be in the limelight?"
   (Sweetly) "My dear, it's very simple," said I. "Both Signor
Caruso and Mr. Charlie Chaplin like to dine and dine well.
And since I am a chef dedicated to quality, they seek me out
and when I am in their presence, some of the limelight naturally glows on me. And I must respond like a gentleman, like
an artist. Yes, one proud of his calling.

(Taking the limelight.)

   A chef I suppose can be a celebrity with the best of them.
I've been filmed, photographed like the best of them; decorated. And like any creative person I've known the thrill of
discovery and the joy of making others happy.
   Delphine was not always so critical of my calling. In fact, I
think, at first, she fancied it. In France for a man to cook
professionally is a most laudable thing—and not unprofitable.
Besides, a chef who's wooing a lady has advantages other men
may not, unless they are poets. Because, you see, like poets
we can concoct personalized and delicate rhapsodies for the

objects of our affections.

(Excitedly) Once, for Delphine, I created *Bombe Nero*, which according to some authorities is my most famous culinary invention: a vanilla mousse and dark–chocolate ice–cream mold covered in merinque. And over it all you pour flaming rum to resemble Nero's burning of Rome. A wild concoction which I might like to serve up this moment if I wasn't afraid of exciting myself too greatly—or Delphine.

(In a brittle voice:) "What are you doing with the flaming liquor, Auguste? You're supposed to be resting, retired . . ."

(Confidentially) I've recently been thinking about a flaming omelet, just like that Bombe. Ah—but I've sent enough omelets into the world. Anyway, Giroix in Paris, *he* was the omelet king. *(Turns to the table.)*

So sad about Giroix. Just before he died he had taken over the kitchen at the Hermitage Hotel one of the best here in Monte Carlo—and the busiest. Gamblers must also eat, you know.

Oh, speak of compulsion again, there's a fatal brand of it: gambling. *(He looks at the unopened telegram on the table.)* And yet— don't we all gamble every day, even a chef like me, an old retired chef. Why, I'd be gambling now with Mme. Giroix just to open this telegram. I mean, I'd be gambling if I had a compulsion to wallow in kitchen fat.

(He toys with something on his desk, then impulsively returns to the table, picks up the telegram and hurriedly opens it.)

(Briefly glancing over the telegram)

Dear me . . . dear me . . . *(Eases into his chair, fully concentrated on the telegram.)*

(Finally addressing the audience)

The young Prince of Wales is coming to the Hermitage! David Edward—old Bertie's grandson. Here. And they want a special dinner for him.

Bertie's grandson, imagine! I've heard a lot about the fellow. Elegant sort. Will want a nice dinner. His father, King George

V, has rather simple tastes I must say. Adores cream cheese. I remember substituting some of it for ice–cream in a coupe I made for him, covered in apricot sauce. Quite good . . .

(Studies the telegram once more.)

This young prince, however, who knows? Probably craves something "jazzy", isn't that the word? Hmm—Bertie's grandson, here in Monte Carlo. No wonder Mme. Giroix is so impatient. César would be climbing the walls. "Ah, we must conceive something original, Auguste, something new. An absolutely new creation!"

(He rises and begins pacing nervously)

A new creation, eh? What? Frog's Legs? No—by now that's almost standard fare. Peach Melba, the same. Well, what does it matter. I don't plan to be there. *(Stops)*

Of course, I could go down just to help set up the kitchen, outline a menu . . .

Bah! But when I get into a kitchen it's like a child in a toy shop. No! Bertie's grandson will have to survive without me.

(Turns to the table and the photographs.)

Brings back memories though. The Prince of Wales. Planning royal shindigs and fancy dishes. *(Shakes his head annoyed.)* That fellow Proust was right. It was that pear! I shouldn't have eaten that pear. That's what started me thinking, remembering all the people and the recipes. They've become one and the same for me: Peach Melba, Eggs Bernhardt, Lamb Edward VII, even sauce Escoffier. Even I've become just a sauce, like César is just a word in the dictionary and a wrong word too!

And how will they remember this new prince? By what dish or concoction?

Well—if *I* create it, maybe . . .Something in an omelet perhaps. A flaming omelet, combining the simplicity of the egg with *le jazz hot* . . . *(Breaks off)*

Oh, now let me be sensible, let me think! What are the factors against my calling Mme. Giroix and succumbing to her blandishments; what? *(Sits)*

A) I'm old. B) I'm tired. C) I've given birth to enough new recipes, especially for an omelet—although a *flaming* omelet . . . *(Annoyed at his distraction.)* D) My devoted wife will not endure it. E) César Ritz would laugh and call me compulsive, a subject about which he is an expert. And F) I am—growing allergic to the heat of the stove!

Now compared to that, what compels? What? The money? Nonsense. The honor? *(Shrugs)* The debt of friendship to my friends the Giroixs, well yes. That's not incidental. *(Emphatically)* But if they are friends, they'll understand. So what? The love of cooking and food? I don't deny that factor. How could I, it's been my life, my passion—my cause!

(Shrinks back in his chair.)

Careful! Causes can kill. Remember Vatel! Remember César Ritz!

Then what? *What* compels me? *(Ponders)*

Bertie's grandson? Maybe for that? For the memories? All the "unsubstantial but still persistent flavors, tastes, ancedotes and incidents . . ."

(After a moment, he rises excitedly)

All right, César. Start laughing! You've won!

(He races to his desk and puts on his toque, grabbing a folder and pen.)

Now, it is absolutely essential, as César would say, to get the menu written down on paper. Plan it all out, nothing left to chance.

(Takes up a sheet of paper and begins to write:)

We'll have a basic seven–course dinner, not a morsel more. Ah ha, I have it. I shall base it on that delicious banquet we gave in Paris to avenge ourselves on the Siege. With one variation: an omelet, a flaming omelet named for the Prince of Wales. *Or* for his lady. Does he have a lady? *(Thinks)* —No, no. He's a bachelor. *(Alerted)*

A bachelor! Ah!—I shall call it *Omelet Célibataire,* combining the simple joys of bachelorhood: eggs, a bit of cream cheese, some fruit. *And* the more flagrant joys, with a dash of flaming brandy. *(Writes feverishly)*

Omelet Wales! (Stops writing) No! *Omelet Jazz!!* Yes, a "jazz" omelet to crown my career. Ooh, la, la. *(Reaches for the telephone) (Looking toward the portrait near the wall)* That's right, laugh César, laugh! But always remember . . . *(Lifts the telephone receiver)* "Good cooking is the absolute foundation of true happiness", to quote Chevalier Georges Auguste Escoffier!

(Talking proudly into the receiver)

Hello, operator? Operator . . . I want to speak to the Hermitage Hotel. Mme. Jean Giroix . . . In the kitchen!

(Quick fade to black.)

THE END

Pronunciation Guide to Difficult Words:

Georges Auguste Escoffier—Jorj Ogŏost Es-kŏf-fee-ay
Jean Giroix—Jhan Jĕer-wah
Trompe Chasseur—Tromp Shă-soor
César—Say-sah
Poularde Derby—Poo-lard Dar-bee
Oeufs Bernhardt—Uh-f Burn-hahr
D'Oyly-Carte—Doilly-Cart
les cuisses de nymphes à l'aurore—lay kwees de neemfs alor-
rŏar
Brillat-Savarin—Bree-yăt-Sav-a-răn
Carême—Kar-em
Coupe—Coop
Delphine—Del-feen
Bombe Nero—Bom Nee-roh
Omelet Celibataire—Om-a-lay Sell-ee-ba-tĕar

Sound Effects

Doorbell chimes
Garden sounds (optional).

Prop List

Telegrams and letters in envelopes—all are practical.

Tea cup and saucer—drinkable tea.

Framed free–standing photographs of King Edward VII; Dame Nellie Melba; Sarah Bernhardt; a young soldier of War I.

An oil portrait, unfinished, on an easel. Portait is of César (a blond, balding man of the 1890's, with mutton-chop moustache). It is at first covered with a piece of gauze.

Thick manuscript tied with ribbon (Cookbook).

A chef's toque (Pastry style).

A cut–glass bowl with fruit—pears are practical.

A finely bound book (Volume I of Proust)—practical.

Artist's supplies (brushes, oil cans, palette, rags).

Writing paper in folder.

Pen in an ink well.

Telephone, circa 1920.

Wastepaper basket near desk.

Scenic Elements Used as Props

Celebrity photos on the walls, framed: Caruso, Chaplin, Queen Victoria, King George V, others of the period.

Photo portrait of Escoffier in full chef's regalia.

Framed watercolors of flowers (by Escoffier).

Framed awards and citations, including the Chevalier of the Legion of Honor, France (ribboned).

Framed letters and recipes, handwritten.

Framed Proclamation from the President of the French Republic to Escoffier: "Our finest ambassador of taste and tradition . . ." (With Tricolor design and ribbons.)

CPSIA information can be obtained
at www.ICGtesting.com
Printed in the USA
BVHW041301181121
621964BV00011B/365